Read and Play
Tractors
by Jim Pipe

Stargazer Books
Mankato, Minnesota

tractor

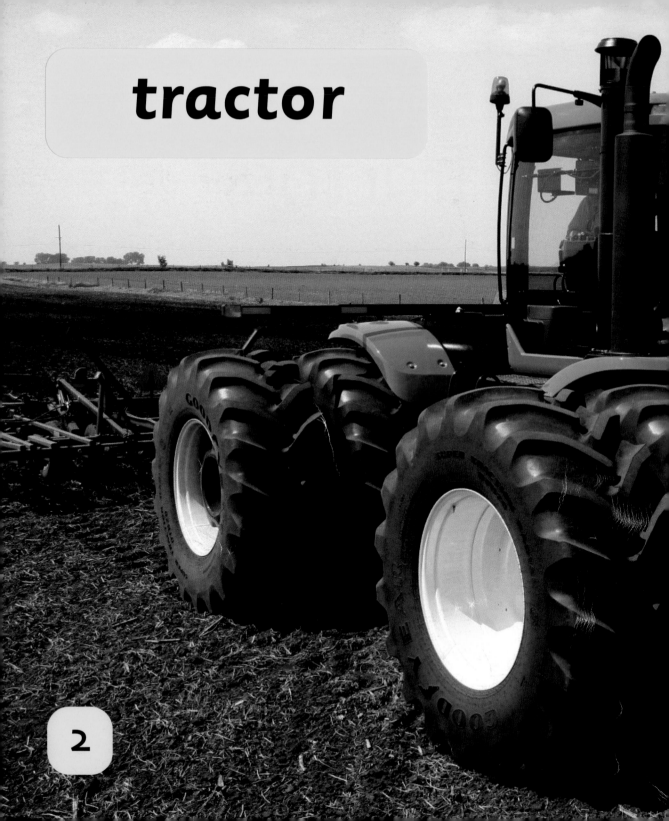

What does a **tractor** do?

pull

4

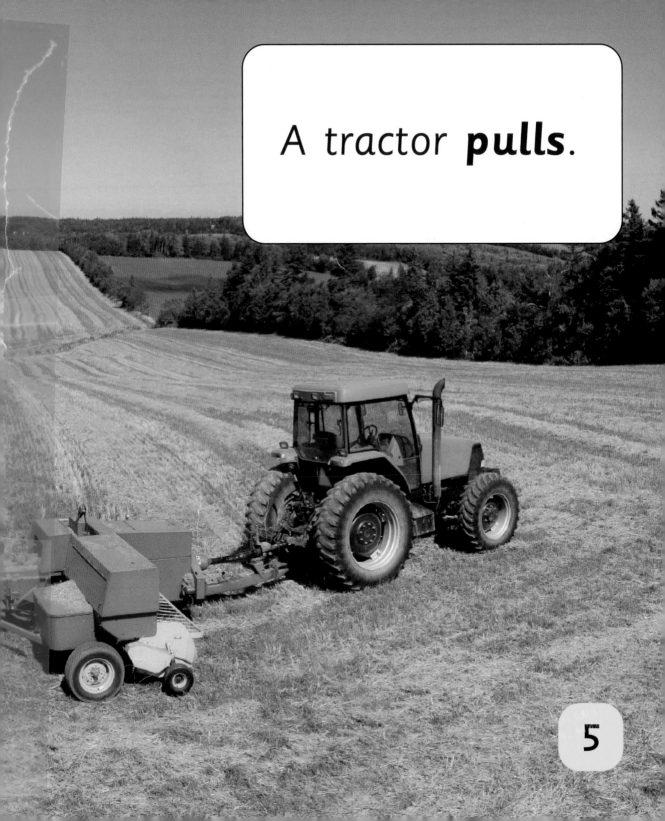

A tractor **pulls**.

5

push

A tractor **pushes**.

7

plant

A tractor **plants** seeds.

9

plow

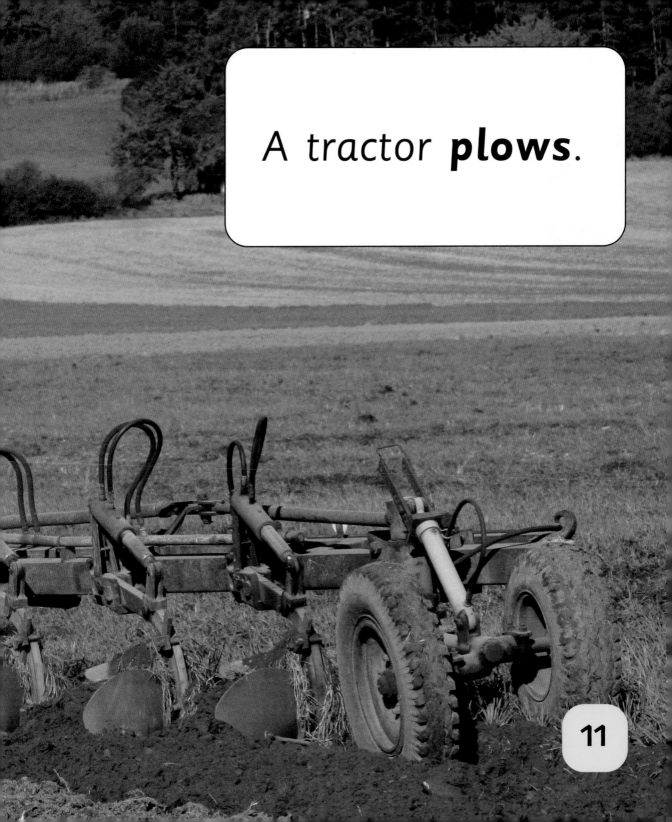

A tractor **plows**.

11

spray

A tractor **sprays**.

13

mow

A tractor **mows**.

15

lift

A tractor **lifts**.

17

clear

18

This tractor **clears** snow.

19

What am I?

driver

engine

wheel

plow

20

Match the words and pictures.

How many?

Can you count the tractors?

21

What job?

22 What are these tractors doing?

Index

23

For Parents and Teachers

Questions you could ask:

p. 2 How many wheels does this tractor have? Eight, though most tractors have four wheels. You could point out the large tires, which help the tractor grip the ground when it is muddy/slippery.

p. 6 Where does the driver sit? In the cab, which is high up so the driver can see all around. The tractor here is piling up silage, grassy plants stored for cattle to eat during the winter.

p. 8 Where do you think the seeds are stored? The seeds are in the yellow buckets which this machine, known as a seed drill, drops onto the ground.

p. 10 Can you see the plow? What do you think it does? As a tractor pulls a plow, it digs long grooves in the soil called furrows that a farmer uses to plant (sow) seeds.

p. 12 Can you see the clouds of spray? The tractor sprays the crops with chemicals to stop weeds from growing and to stop insects from eating the crops.

p. 14 Where have you seen a mower? Mowing means cutting grass, e.g. lawnmower. When the grass is cut it dries out and is known as hay.

p. 16 What is this tractor lifting? The tractor is lifting a hay bale, which is used to feed animals such as cattle and sheep during the winter.

p. 18 How does the tractor clear the snow? It pushes it out of the way like a bulldozer then sprays the snow away from the road.

Activities you could do:

• Organize a visit to a farm and watch a tractor at work, e.g. plowing. Give each child a printed checklist to tick off the things they might see on the farm, e.g. animals, buildings, machines.

• Plan a day when children bring toy tractors into school. Ask them to describe all the different jobs the tractor can do, e.g. pushing, pulling, lifting and tipping loads, plowing, planting seeds, mowing.

• Decorate a farm mural on a large piece of paper. Children can draw farm animals, tractors, barns etc.

• Introduce farms through songs such as "Old Macdonald" or "Baa Baa Black Sheep."

© Aladdin Books Ltd 2009

Designed and produced by
Aladdin Books Ltd

First published in 2009 in the United States by
Stargazer Books,
distributed by
Black Rabbit Books
PO Box 3263
Mankato, MN 56002

Library of Congress Cataloging-in-Publication Data

Pipe, Jim, 1966-
  Tractors / Jim Pipe.
    p. cm. -- (Read and play)
  Includes bibliographical references and index.
  Summary: "In very simple language and photographs, describes tractors. Includes quizzes and games"--Provided by publisher.
    ISBN 978-1-59604-183-7
  1. Tractors--Juvenile literature. I. Title.
  TL233.15.P57 2009
  629.225'2--dc22

                        2008015289

Series consultant
Zoe Stillwell is an experienced preschool teacher.

Photocredits:
l-left, r-right, b-bottom, t-top, c-center, m-middle.
All photos istockphoto.com except:
2-3, 14-15, 16-17, 20br, 22tl & br, 23tml, ml & br—courtesy New Holland. 8-9, 12-13 , 18-19, 21, 22bl, 23tl, bml & bmr—courtesy John Deere.